THE
YOUNG PERSON'S
GUIDE TO
CONQUERING THE
WORLD

A GUIDED JOURNAL by the Editors of TEEN VOGUE

Abrams Noterie, New York

WE DEDICATE
THIS JOURNAL TO OUR
TEENAGE SELVES.

I dedicate this journal
to my younger self. Maybe with
it in her hand, she would have
been able to navigate the world
with a bit more ease.

ALISON MAHONEY,
News & Politics Features Editor

Young Claire,
if you had this journal, I like
to think you might have realized
sooner that your body does not
define your dreams, and that you
have so much potential beyond
trying to fit into smaller clothing.

CLAIRE DODSON,
Entertainment News Editor

I spent a lot of time
worrying that I was missing
out on something, whether it was
something small, like a party,
or something bigger: the secret
to life. This journal would have
reminded me that there is no
secret. It's all about the journey.

BRITTANY MCNAMARA,
Wellness News Editor

Dear teenage Lindsay,
One day representation and inclusivity will become a reality in fashion, beauty, culture, and all the things you love so dearly. Your mom regularly tells you to be what you need to see. You'll be shocked to learn how those words ring true as your life unfolds.

LINDSAY PEOPLES WAGNER,
Editor-in-Chief

I struggled so much with my body image, confidence, and self-worth. I would have used this as a guide to sort out some of the complicated emotions that come with being a teenager.

ALYSSA HARDY,
Fashion News Editor

I dedicate this book to my teenage self because sometimes you need a guide (other than your parents) to lead you through tough times and give you hope for your future self.

RAJNI JACQUES,
Fashion Director

To the girl who did not know herself and the boy she was trying to be instead: Joy and love will find you. I wish I could've had a chance to know that when I was you.

LUCY DIAVOLO,
News & Politics News Editor

LET'S GET STARTED

Get ready to conquer the world.

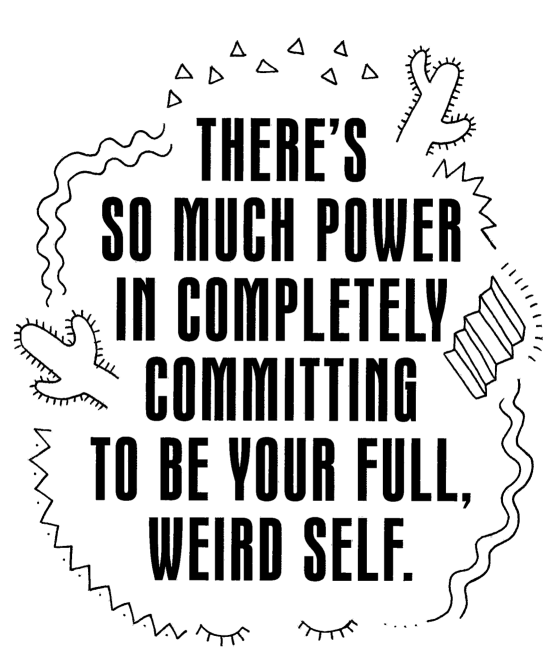

THERE'S
SO MUCH POWER
IN COMPLETELY
COMMITTING
TO BE YOUR FULL,
WEIRD SELF.

MAGGIE ROGERS

YOU'RE PROBABLY REMINDED EVERY DAY BY YOUR TEACHERS, PARENTS, PUBLIC FIGURES, AND MORE THAT TEENS—*YOU!*—ARE THE FUTURE. THIS IS TRUE AND IT'S AN IMPORTANT THING TO REMEMBER, BUT WHAT MANY PEOPLE OFTEN FORGET IS THAT TEENS ARE ALSO THE *NOW.*

They're **leading critical legislation** reform movements across the country and road tripping to Washington, DC, to participate in meaningful marches. They're using social media to push conversation surrounding the **body positivity movement** and to champion the **importance of self-care**. They're standing up for human rights and challenging the government's most powerful players. Many are doing this despite the fact they can't even vote yet!

Your power to make a difference doesn't start when you're eighteen or when you have one hundred thousand Instagram followers listening to what you have to say. It starts when you decide to **get to know yourself** and what really matters to you, as that is the first step toward **intentional change**. These pages are an excellent place to begin. It may not be easy, but it will be worth it!

A PROMISE TO YOURSELF

Ultimately, what you're able to get out of this journal is one hundred percent up to you. It will depend on your honesty and the thought you put into it. Write a pledge to yourself to define how you plan to approach this journey. Whenever you're in need of a little motivation, flip to this page.

By starting this journal, I pledge to write the rule book for my own life.

When I write about myself, I will make an effort to:

1

_____

_____

_____

If I freeze up because of self-criticism, I will remind myself that:

2

_____

_____

_____

When I hear the words "conquer the world," the first thing that comes to my mind is:

3

_____

_____

_____

_____

NAME   DATE

SO, WHAT'S AHEAD?

Each chapter in this journal centers
on a different topic that you'll be asked to explore.
By doing so, you'll become more in tune with yourself
and your goals than ever and will feel empowered
to tackle whatever life throws at you. Here's the
road map to a new sense of confidence
in all areas of your life.

CHAPTER 01:

GIRL UNFILTERED

Who are you right now? What do you like, what drives you, what are you passionate about? Pour yourself into this chapter and allow it to serve as a snapshot of your current singular self. Be honest and don't hold back. Believe us, your older self will thank you for it someday.

CHAPTER 02:

FAMILY MATTERS

Who do you come from? Respecting and understanding your family members and their traditions is important, but so is allowing yourself to become your own person. In this chapter, you'll navigate this dichotomy and spend time with your loved ones along the way.

CHAPTER 03:

YOUR RIDE-OR-DIES

Who are your chosen ones? From support systems to sounding boards, your friends play numerous roles in your life. This chapter will help you honor them, get to know them more deeply, and learn how you can best show up for one another.

CHAPTER 04:

BODY PARTY

How do you celebrate yourself? Sing your body's praises and recognize all that it does for you on a daily basis. This chapter will be a step toward erasing areas of shame that prevent you from loving yourself wholly.

CHAPTER 05:

STRESS LESS

How do you soothe yourself? Everyone needs to check in with themselves every now and again. Along with providing tools to help manage stress and anxiety, this chapter encourages you to unplug, get creative, and take some time for yourself.

CHAPTER 06:

RAISE YOUR VOICE

How will you be heard? Here's where you'll home in on the issues that matter most to you and figure out how you can get involved with them. It'll serve as a reminder of the actions you want to take and give you the confidence to speak up.

CHAPTER 07:

FUTURE THINKING

What are your dreams and goals? Thinking about the future is overwhelming, but the trick is to toggle your mind between the long game and the small decisions you make each day. Define what you genuinely want, use your imagination, and use these pages to set your compass.

CONCLUSION:

THIS IS NOT THE END

Where will you go from here? At this point, you'll have completed an entire book of exercises that have challenged, enlightened, and empowered you. You'll be ready to go forth and conquer the world—but not before a little reflection about everything you've gained.

CHAPTER 01

GIRL UNFILTERED

Who are you right now?

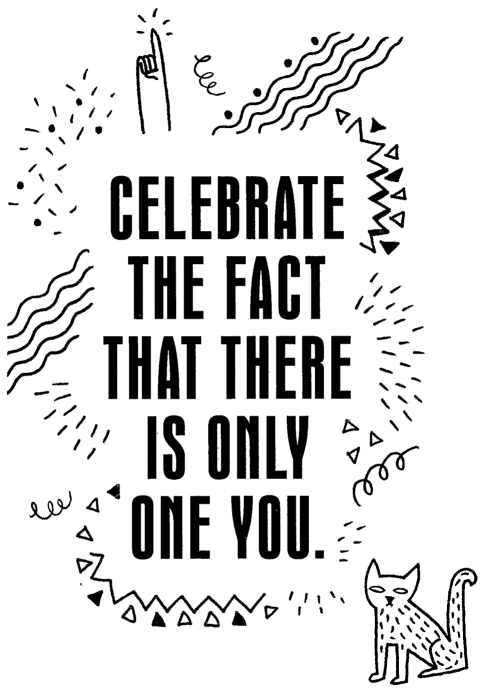

CELEBRATE THE FACT THAT THERE IS ONLY ONE YOU.

SHAY MITCHELL

WHO ARE YOU? IT'S A QUESTION YOU'LL SPEND YOUR WHOLE LIFE TRYING TO FIGURE OUT—AND THERE'S NEVER JUST ONE WAY TO ANSWER. HOW DO YOU SPEND YOUR TIME? WHAT DO YOU STAND FOR? WHAT MAKES YOU TICK, WHAT DO YOU LOVE, AND HOW CAN YOU MAKE A LASTING IMPACT ON THE WORLD?

All of these things and more—your favorites, pet peeves, talents, dreams, desires, and even your shortcomings—make you exactly who you are. Let's revel in that. You are an **inimitable force of nature** who will navigate life and its challenges in your own way. In short, your power lies in your **vast and sparkling you-ness**.

In this section, you'll get all the basics down so you can use them as the building blocks for **your future wins**. You won't know where you can go without also standing firm in where you've been, and no one knows those answers better than you. When you turn to this chapter years from now it will be like **opening up a precious time capsule**—you'll be able to look back at a past version of yourself and understand how the *who you were* transformed into *the who you are*.

SELFIE PORTRAIT

Fill in the blank phone screen in whatever way feels most authentic to you, so that it serves as a snapshot of who you are right now. It doesn't matter if it's a self-portrait, a pasted-in photograph, an autobiographical poem, or a single word—so long as you feel it captures your essence, any type of creative expression is fair game.

#MOOD

Create a visual mood board to express your aesthetic. Gather words, images, colors, and textures and make a collage here.

MY MANIFESTO

Fill in the blanks with the first words or phrases
that come to mind. Don't overthink it!
It doesn't matter if the end result is half-serious
and half-ridiculous. Just choose the words
that make sense for you.

Three words I would use to describe myself are _____ ,

_____ , and _____ .

The most important thing about my identity is my _____ .

When I was _____ , I discovered my greatest passion, which is

_____ . It makes me feel

_____ , and completely _____ my soul.

Right now, my biggest personal goal is to _____ .

I know I can achieve it because I _____ .

On a larger scale, I want to _____ .

This is important to me because _____ .

My friends would tell you I am _____ .

When we hang out I feel like I'm the _____ one in the group.

My day-to-day life is filled with _____ .

I love eating _____ and watching _____ ,

and my favorite song right now is _____ .

I am _____ and I will never give up on

_____ . I have the power to _____ .

THE PROUSTEEN QUESTIONNAIRE

In 1886, at the age of fourteen, Marcel Proust (renowned French essayist and novelist) filled out a questionnaire with prompts specifically designed to reveal **the true nature of the participant.** His answers were so remarkable that they would eventually inspire one of the most widely completed personality tests of all time, now known as the **Proust Questionnaire**.

A **popular type of parlor game** in the late nineteenth century, such questionnaires were taken by everyone from German philosopher **Karl Marx** to French painter **Paul Cézanne**. The tradition continues on the pages of *Vanity Fair*, where the Proust Questionnaire has been completed by modern icons including **David Bowie** and **Cecile Richards**. Follow in their footsteps and fill in your own answers.

1. What is your idea of perfect happiness?

_____

2. What is your greatest fear?

_____

3. What is the trait you most deplore in yourself?

_____

4. What is the trait you most deplore in others?

_____

5. Which living person do you most admire?

_____

6. What is your greatest extravagance?

_____

7. What is your current state of mind?

_____

8. What do you consider the most overrated virtue?

_____

9. On what occasion do you lie?

_____

10. Which living person do you most despise?

_____

11. What is the quality you most like in a person?

_____

12. Which words or phrases do you most overuse?

_____

13. What or who is the greatest love of your life?

_____

14. When and where were you happiest?

_____

15. Which talent would you most like to have?

_____

16. If you could change one thing about yourself, what would it be?

_____

17. What do you consider your greatest achievement?

_____

18. If you were to die and come back as a person or a thing, what would it be?

_____

19. Where would you most like to live?

_____

20. What is your most treasured possession?

_____

21. What do you regard as the lowest depth of misery?

_____

22. What is your favorite occupation?

_____

23. What is your most marked characteristic?

_____

24. What do you most value in your friends?

_____

25. Who are your favorite writers?

_____

26. Who is your hero of fiction?

_____

27. Which historical figure do you most identify with?

_____

28. Who are your heroes in real life?

_____

29. What are your favorite names?

_____

30. What is your greatest regret?

_____

31. How would you like to die?

_____

32. What is your motto?

_____

FAVES

Some favorite reads

A playlist of favorite songs

Who you're following on social media

TRUTH BOMB

We've all got secrets.
Think of a particularly weighty one you've
been harboring and write it down on this
blue page, in blue ink. It won't be visible,
but just writing it down is a cathartic
way to unburden yourself.

RAD
SELF-ACCEPTANCE

Recognizing our weaknesses and loving ourselves in spite of them is one of the most radical things we can do for ourselves. Jot down one habit or tendency that you want to work on over the next year and why. Remember that change doesn't happen overnight.

One thing I want to work on:

_____

_____

I want to work on this because:

_____

_____

_____

_____

_____

_____

_____

EMBRACE WHAT MAKES YOU UNIQUE EVEN IF IT MAKES OTHERS UNCOMFORTABLE.

JANELLE MONÁE

THE MAGIC THREE

Individuality is what makes each and every one of us so interesting and cool. We should never be ashamed of our singularity; the world would be hopelessly boring if we were all the same. So it's time to let your freak flag fly! Write down three things about yourself that are either unexpected or wonderfully weird.

Something you're really into that would surprise others:

1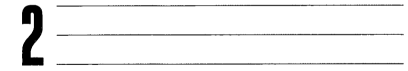

Something you like wearing (or would wear), even if it means getting teased:

2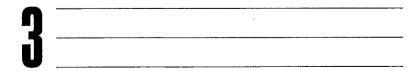

Something quirky about the way you express yourself (words you love, hand gestures, the way you move):

3

CHAPTER 02

FAMILY MATTERS

Who do you come from?

FAMILY CREATES A SAFE PLACE.

DREW BARRYMORE

FAMILY IS WHERE YOU COME FROM.
IT'S SOMETHING TO HONOR, RESPECT,
APPRECIATE, AND KNOW DEEPLY. AND
WHILE FAMILY PROFOUNDLY SHAPES YOU
AS AN INDIVIDUAL, IT DOESN'T DEFINE YOU—
ULTIMATELY, YOU HAVE THE POWER TO DO
THAT FOR YOURSELF.

Family takes on various roles over the course of our lives. For many, it's those that have raised us, from bike lessons to college move-in days. But at its core, family is the people that have **stuck with us when things are the hardest**—whether that's family by blood or the family we have found over the years—and that push and inspire us to be **the best people we can be**.

Leaning into your heritage, familial traditions, and the advice that loved ones give you is so important. But it's also important to follow **your own heart,** invest in your own ideas and beliefs, and chase your own dreams, even if they go against the grain of what your family might expect. In this chapter, you'll do a deep dive into your family history and **connect with family members** in the process, all while cultivating the wisdom to best navigate **your singular path**.

FAMILY TREE

Take a moment to acknowledge the network of people you've been connected to since birth: your family. Draw your family tree and include however many generations you'd like. Include your fuzzy friends, too.

MAD PROPS

Whom do you look up to and why?

Write a letter to a family member you admire and list all the ways they inspire and influence you. Doing this will remind you of the traits you want to embody yourself. Once you're done, take a picture of this page and text it to the recipient.

DEAR _____,

_____

_____

_____

_____

_____

_____

_____

_____

_____

_____

_____

_____

_____

_____

_____

_____

LOVE, _____

DATE _____ / _____ / _____

DISH IT

Choose one of your favorite family recipes
and find out how to make it. Jot down the recipe,
including the ingredients list and instructions.
Then try making the dish yourself and inviting
your family to share. If it doesn't work out,
you can always order pizza. It's the
effort that counts!

INGREDIENTS

INSTRUCTIONS

WISDOM DROP

Interview one of your parents, grandparents, or favorite relatives.
You might want to record their answers on your phone, and then later you can jot down the quotes you loved best. It'll give you a chance to think about what surprised you most about this conversation.

1. Tell me about your childhood best friend. How did you meet? What was their name? What's one of your favorite memories with them?

_____

_____

_____

_____

2. What was your favorite thing about the city you grew up in? What was your least favorite?

_____

_____

_____

_____

3. What was one of your biggest stressors as a teen, and how did you ultimately handle it?

_____

_____

_____

_____

4. Were you ever compelled to get involved with a political or social cause? If so, what was it and why? If not, do you wish you had been?

_____

_____

_____

_____

5. When have you felt most at peace and happy with life?

_____

_____

_____

_____

6. Why did you decide to pursue the career you did? Are you happy with your choice?

_____

_____

_____

_____

7. Looking back, if you could've done one thing differently when you were younger, what would it be?

_____

_____

_____

_____

I ♥ MY PEOPLE

Write little notes of gratitude to your family members simply because they're always there for you. Cut out the tiny cards on the opposite page, write messages on the back, and place them on pillows, by the coffee maker, or wherever someone will be surprised to find them.

FLASHBACK

Sift through your favorite memories involving your family and choose the one that sticks out to you the most. Write about it below, describing why you love it so much. If you'd prefer to draw the memory, that's cool, too.

SAME, BUT DIFFERENT

Relating to your family and sharing in various interests, traditions, and ideas is important, but so is individuality and feeling free to express your selfhood. Fill in the blanks opposite with the ways you differentiate yourself from your family. Always remember that there's power in uniqueness!

At first glance, the most obvious difference you would notice between me

and my family is _____. In reality,

the thing I feel most sets me apart is _____

_____ .

My parents aren't ready to let me _____ ,

but I feel ready because _____ .

While my family and I like to _____ together,

I prefer to _____ on my own.

My family and I all share the belief that _____

_____.

But when my family is talking about _____ ,

I notice that I feel differently about it. I believe _____

_____.

Despite our differences, I appreciate that our family dynamic is _____

_____.

Family is _____

_____.

TO BE HONEST, IT ALL COMES DOWN TO FAMILY.

TROYE SIVAN

THE MAGIC THREE

From the time we are born, all of our information about ourselves and the world is filtered through our family. As you grow up, it is important to see and understand the culture of your family and to celebrate it (but not necessarily conform to it). Write down three important takeaways about your family.

A family member who has a huge influence on me:

A tradition that I want to carry on:

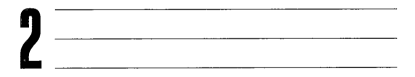

A belief or drive that is unique to me:

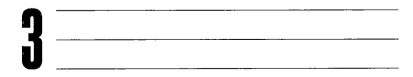

CHAPTER 03

YOUR RIDE -OR- DIES

Who are your chosen ones?

MY FRIENDS ARE MY ESTATE. FORGIVE ME THEN THE AVARICE TO HOARD THEM.

EMILY DICKINSON

WHO WOULD WE BE WITHOUT OUR FRIENDS, OUR PLATONIC SOULMATES, OUR PARTNERS IN CRIME? WITHOUT THEM, WHO WOULD LISTEN TO OUR INNERMOST SECRETS? WHO WOULD LAUGH WITH US UNTIL WE FELL OVER? WHO WOULD WE DO ANYTHING FOR?

As you embark on a journey to conquer the world, you need the **right people behind you**. Friendships will nurture and sustain you as you progress toward your goals. If you fall off course, your friends will remind you **why you started in the first place**. When obstacles start to weigh you down, they'll **encourage you not to quit**. And when you finally achieve the life you've dreamed of, your friends will be there **cheering the loudest**—because they know exactly **what it took to get there**.

"My friends are my estate." That's how famed poet Emily Dickinson described the monumental importance of her **inner circle**. In this chapter, you'll be asked to think about the roles your friendships have played in your own life. Who are the **major pillars in your life**? How do you, in turn, support those pillars? You'll even be asked to get your gang together to create something, so be prepared for **major bonding ahead**. Home (or your estate!) is where your heart is.

BFF WALL OF FAME

Doodle* a picture of your friends in the frames below and write a "most likely to" superlative underneath each. What qualities make each person exceptionally rad?

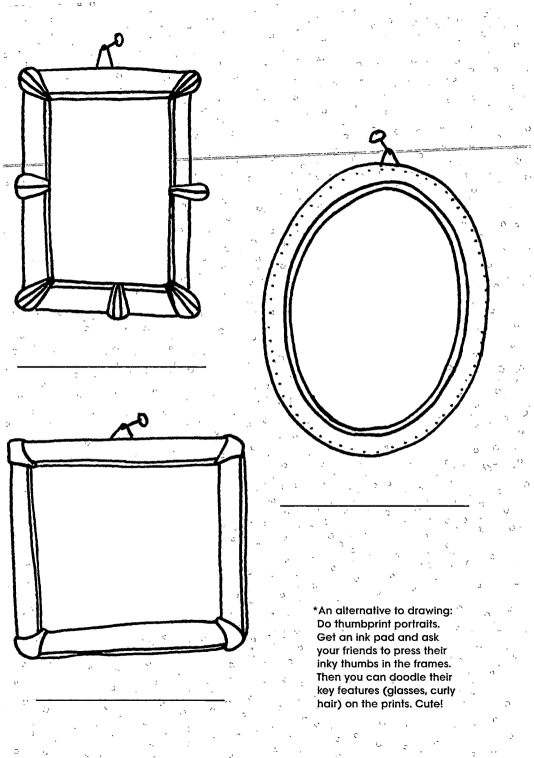

*An alternative to drawing:
Do thumbprint portraits.
Get an ink pad and ask
your friends to press their
inky thumbs in the frames.
Then you can doodle their
key features (glasses, curly
hair) on the prints. Cute!

HOW WELL DO YOU KNOW EACH OTHER?

The next two pages are **identical quizzes** for **you** and **your best friend**. Remove them both and sit down together to fill in the prompts. **Your own answers** to the questions go on one side, and the responses that you **think your best friend would write** go on the other. Once you're done, swap papers and compare notes.

8–11 correct: Do you two have ESP or something?
5–8 correct: Not bad, but more deep talks are in order.
0–4 correct: Did you two just meet?!

ABOUT ME: _____

NAME

My first concert was:

_____

If I could go anywhere for my next vacation it would be:

_____

My biggest fear is:

_____

If I were to get a tattoo, it would be:

_____ on my: _____

I spend a lot of free time on:

_____

My current crush is:

_____

My favorite snack is:

_____

The celebrity I'm most obsessed with right now is:

_____

My favorite color is:

_____

Career-wise, I want to be:

_____

A word that I use a lot is:

_____

ABOUT MY BFF: _____
NAME

My bestie's first concert was:

_____

If my BFF could go anywhere for their next vacation it would be:

_____

My bestie's biggest fear is:

_____

If my BFF were to get a tattoo, it would be:

_____ on their: _____

My bestie spends a lot of free time on:

_____

My BFF's current crush is:

_____

My bestie's favorite snack is:

_____

The celebrity my BFF is obsessed with right now is:

_____

My bestie's favorite color is:

_____

Career-wise, my BFF wants to be:

_____

A word that my bestie uses a lot is:

_____

ABOUT ME: _____

NAME

My first concert was:

_____

If I could go anywhere for my next vacation it would be:

_____

My biggest fear is:

_____

If I were to get a tattoo, it would be:

_____ on my: _____

I spend a lot of free time on:

_____

My current crush is:

_____

My favorite snack is:

_____

The celebrity I'm most obsessed with right now is:

_____

My favorite color is:

_____

Career-wise, I want to be:

_____

A word that I use a lot is:

_____

ABOUT MY BFF: _____

My bestie's first concert was:

_____

If my BFF could go anywhere for their next vacation it would be:

_____

My bestie's biggest fear is:

_____

If my BFF were to get a tattoo, it would be:

_____ on their: _____

My bestie spends a lot of free time on:

_____

My BFF's current crush is:

_____

My bestie's favorite snack is:

_____

The celebrity my BFF is obsessed with right now is:

_____

My bestie's favorite color is:

_____

Career-wise, my BFF wants to be:

_____

A word that my bestie uses a lot is:

_____

FRIEND REQUEST

Those who live by the phrase "no new friends" are seriously missing out. Yes, new friends—the more, the better! Think of someone you are friend-crushing on and ask them something about themselves that will help you get to know them on a deeper level. Write their name and answer here.

Name:

_____

Question:

_____

_____

_____

_____

Answer:

_____

_____

_____

_____

THROW-BACK FRIEND

Friends come and go in life, and that's OK!
Whether because of a cross-country move
or simply because you two grew apart, chances
are you've lost touch with an old BFF. Think
back to a favorite memory involving someone
you no longer hang out with and write
down why this memory has stuck with you.
When you remember what someone
added to your life, no relationship
ever truly ends.

KEEP IT 100

It's natural to feel hurt or angered at times by something a friend did or said. The most important thing is how you handle these feelings. Write a letter to someone whose actions have bothered you. Whether you give your friend the letter or not is totally your call. Sometimes just acknowledging your feelings puts you on the path to forgiveness.

DEAR _____,

_____

_____

_____

_____

_____

_____

_____

_____

_____

_____

_____

_____

SINCERELY, _____

DATE _____ / _____ / _____

EXQUISITE CORPSE

Group project! Gather four or five friends;
you're going to write a story with each person
contributing one sentence at a time. Choose someone
to write the first sentence. Then pass the journal
to the next person to add their contribution.
Before passing it to the third person, cover the
writing with a piece of paper, so that only
the last sentence is visible. Continue passing
the journal around until the page is full,
and then read the hilariously disjointed
tale all the way through.

MY GREATEST WISH FOR EVERY YOUNG PERSON IS A FRIEND WHO CAN TRAVEL THE WORLD, CHANGE THE COURSE OF HISTORY, AND STILL BE THERE FOR YOU THROUGH THICK AND THIN.

BETSY EBELING
Hillary Clinton's BFF

THE MAGIC THREE

Female friendship is so powerful, especially when it involves women who build up, cheer on, and applaud their fellow girl gang members. Write down the ways in which you and your girls show up for one another.

My friend(s) supported me when:

1 _____
_____
_____

I show my support by:

2 _____
_____
_____

I'm proud of how we interact because:

3 _____
_____
_____

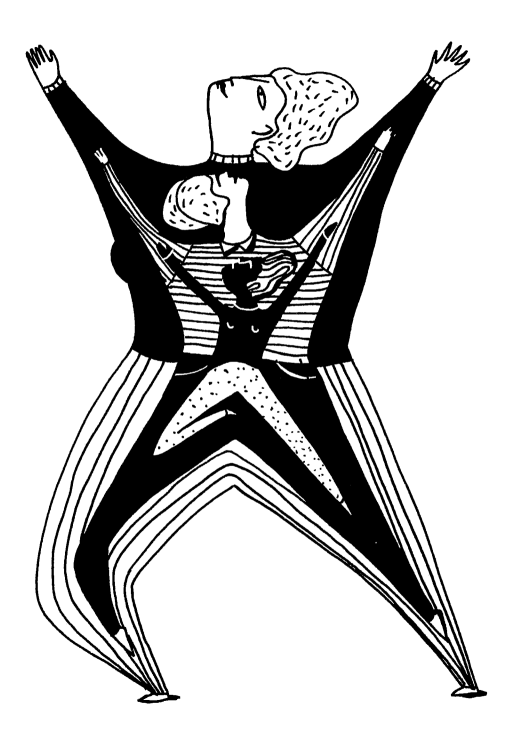

CHAPTER 04

BODY PARTY

How do you celebrate yourself?

WE DESERVE TO LOVE OURSELVES FOR WHO WE ARE.

JAZZ JENNINGS

DOES ANY ASPECT OF OURSELVES DREDGE UP MORE INSECURITIES, PUBLIC OPINIONS, AND SELF-CRITICISM THAN OUR BODIES? AND YET, THESE WEIRD LITTLE SHAPES WE LIVE IN ALSO ARE OUR CHANCE TO BE IN THE WORLD, TO CHALLENGE THE SPACES WE ENTER AND THE PHYSICAL SPACE WE'RE ALLOWED TO TAKE UP.

It's time to do away with the **unrealistic standards** and shame that oppress the body and to celebrate the things that make it the powerful figure it is. **Let's talk about periods**. Let's take pride in our **silvery stretch marks**. Let's embrace our curves, or lack thereof. Let's be the ones to decide **our own definition of beautiful**.

This chapter will ask you to **reconnect with your body** and take some time to appreciate it and all that it does. You'll acknowledge the things that make it so **singularly special**, while also **reflecting on bodies in general** and the way you perceive and talk about them. In writing about all the ways you love your body and all bodies, you'll help to **erase the unfair stigmas** surrounding it.

BODY LANGUAGE

Our bodies are so much more than their shape!
Circle any of the words you're proudest to embody below
and write in a few more that are specific to you.

REGAL

HANDY

Graceful

STRONG

Flexible

WARM

DEAR BODY

Choose one part or aspect of your body
that you've been especially hard on and write
a letter to it. Start off by identifying why you
were taught to believe it wasn't beautiful,
and then show it some love by apologizing
for ever putting it down and listing a few things
you love about it. Whether you choose a
certain curve, a rippling of stretch marks,
a scar, or cellulite, it deserves to be
accepted and embraced.

DEAR _____ ,

_____

_____

_____

_____

_____

_____

_____

_____

_____

_____

_____

_____

_____

_____

_____

LOVE, _____

DATE _____ / _____ / _____

JUST BEACHY

There is no such thing as a bikini-ready body. If you've got a body, it's ready for a bikini. Or a one-piece, tankini, or monokini, for that matter! Draw bathing suits on each of the lounging babes below and prove that every body is a beach body.

IT'S NATURAL.
PERIOD.

It's time we put an end to period shaming!
Menstruating is a normal, natural cycle that happens within many bodies, so why is it still taboo to talk about? Find a female family member or friend and discuss the questions on the opposite page, filling in both of your answers for each one. Hopefully you'll feel emboldened to continue opening up dialogues about periods with others in the future.

1. Tell me the story of when you first got your period and the emotions you were feeling at the time.

_____

_____

_____

_____

_____

2. Does having your period make you feel powerful at all? How so?

_____

_____

_____

_____

_____

3. What are some of your favorite ways to deal with PMS and period pains?

_____

_____

_____

_____

_____

PORTRAIT OF _____

Choose someone you trust and love and draw a picture of them on this page. Don't worry about your artistic skills—the more Picasso-like, the better! Then jot down three things you admire most about your subject.

PORTRAIT OF_____

Choose someone you trust and love and ask them to draw a picture of you. Then have them jot down three things they admire about you. Seeing yourself through another's eyes can totally change your own perception of yourself!

WHEN I FEEL INSECURE, I LOOK IN THE MIRROR AND SAY WHAT I APPRECIATE ABOUT MYSELF.

LULU BONFILS

THE MAGIC THREE

Self-love is especially radical when you practice it in your shakiest and strongest moments alike. Write down a list of the things you love most about yourself and flip to it whenever you need a boost of confidence.

My favorite feature is:

1

I appreciate my body's ability to:

2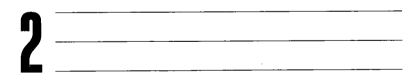

I take pleasure in:

3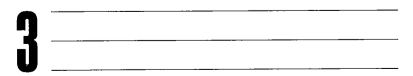

CHAPTER 05

STRESS LESS

How do you soothe yourself?

IT'S OK TO NOT BE OK.

PARIS JACKSON

LIFE IS CHAOTIC AF. BETWEEN BALANCING SCHOOL, A SOCIAL LIFE, HOBBIES, HOMEWORK, AND FAMILY, SO MUCH IS TYPICALLY INVOLVED IN THE DAY-TO-DAY THAT STRESS AND EMOTIONAL VOLATILITY CAN ALMOST FEEL LIKE THE NORM. SOCIAL MEDIA DOESN'T EXACTLY HELP, EITHER. IN FACT, IT CAN BE ONE OF THE GREATEST SOURCES OF DISTRACTION AND ANXIETY.

FOMO is real, and scrolling through people's **highlight reels** all day rather than **seeing their real, flawed lives** can sometimes leave us feeling **inadequate**, jealous, or left out. Taking all of these stressors into account, it's never been more important to schedule **check-ins with ourselves** to make sure we're in a happy and **healthy headspace**.

That's exactly what these next several pages are for. From ways to de-stress and **boost your self-confidence** to activities that simply ask you to **unplug** and spend quality time with yourself and others, this chapter is filled with prompts and activities that you can turn to whenever you're **feeling a little in over your head**. Flip to them anytime you need some help shifting your thoughts to a more positive point of view. Self-love and self-care are signs of a **strong, smart, and determined individual**.

VENT SESSION

Pull out your phone, open your voice recorder app, and hit record. For forty-five seconds, talk about anything and everything that's been bothering you. Get it all off your chest. Then listen to the recording and choose one of your frustrations to think over. On the following page, write the steps you can take to resolve it in a healthy and productive way.

ON A SPECTRUM

Check out these sets of opposing character traits. Mark where you fall on the spectrum between each pair, and then take a moment to reflect on how your results work together collectively to form who you are. There are no right or wrong answers to this exercise!

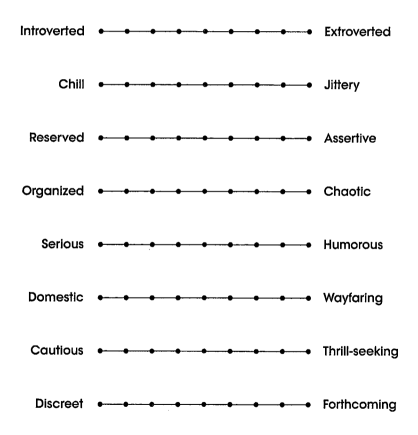

Introverted •———•———•———•———•———•———•———• Extroverted

Chill •———•———•———•———•———•———•———• Jittery

Reserved •———•———•———•———•———•———•———• Assertive

Organized •———•———•———•———•———•———•———• Chaotic

Serious •———•———•———•———•———•———•———• Humorous

Domestic •———•———•———•———•———•———•———• Wayfaring

Cautious •———•———•———•———•———•———•———• Thrill-seeking

Discreet •———•———•———•———•———•———•———• Forthcoming

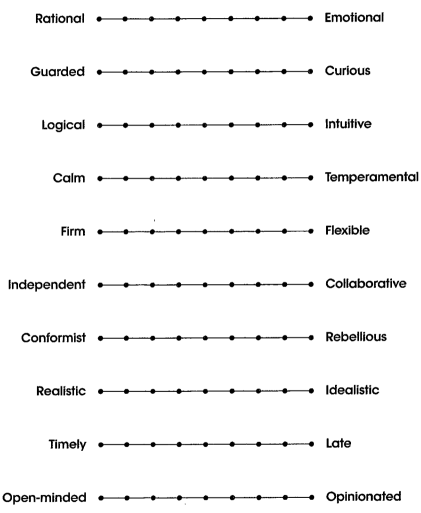

Rational ●————●————●————●————●————●————●————● Emotional

Guarded ●————●————●————●————●————●————●————● Curious

Logical ●————●————●————●————●————●————●————● Intuitive

Calm ●————●————●————●————●————●————●————● Temperamental

Firm ●————●————●————●————●————●————●————● Flexible

Independent ●————●————●————●————●————●————●————● Collaborative

Conformist ●————●————●————●————●————●————●————● Rebellious

Realistic ●————●————●————●————●————●————●————● Idealistic

Timely ●————●————●————●————●————●————●————● Late

Open-minded ●————●————●————●————●————●————●————● Opinionated

DREAM CATCHER

Think of the most vivid dream you've ever had,
or a recurring theme in your dreams, and
write it down here. Underline some key words
and do a little research into dream symbolism.
Any theories about what this dream means?

FREE ASSOCIATIONS

Quick! Draw or jot down
the first thing that comes to mind
when you see these words,
no matter how silly or irrelevant
it might seem.

star

flying

toes

hot dog

fresh

jell-o

obsession

PS: U ROCK

Spreading love to others is a great way

to get into a positive mindset. Cut out these
compliment cards and give them to people who
really should know how awesome they are.

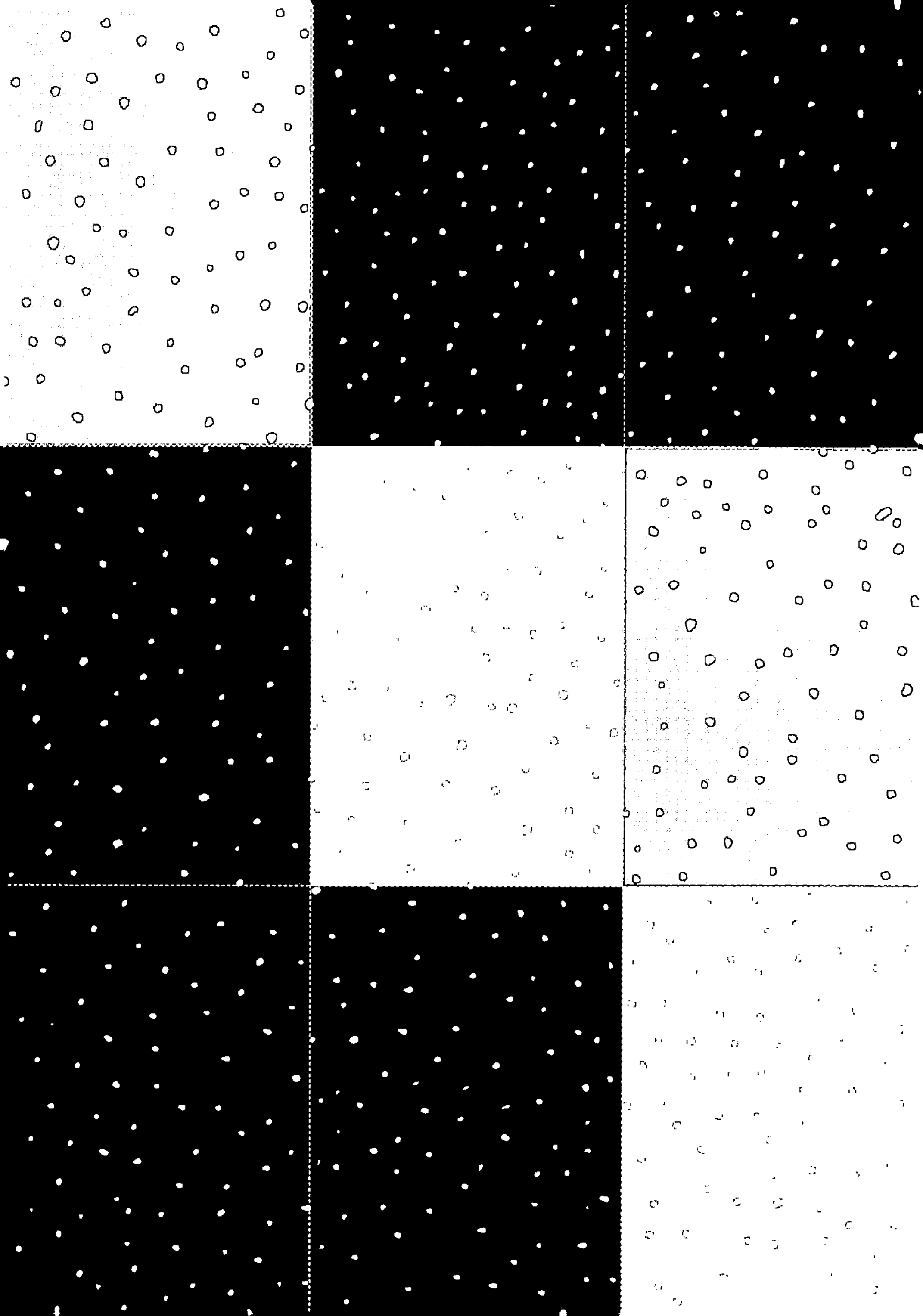

PAY YOURSELF A COMPLIMENT

Put modesty on pause for a second. Forget about external validation and social media likes. Give yourself a pat on the back by answering these three questions.

1. What's something you've done recently that you're proud of?

_____

_____

_____

_____

2. What's your favorite thing about your personality? Why?

_____

_____

_____

3. What's something you know a lot about that you could teach others?

_____

_____

_____

REFRESH SESH

If you're ever feeling overly stressed, anxious, or emotional, take a few minutes to complete one of these three mental health exercises. They'll help you check in with yourself emotionally and get back into a better headspace.

BREATHE

If you're feeling stressed, anxious, or otherwise tense, try the 4-7-8 relaxing breath exercise. Start off by pressing the tip of your tongue on the roof of your mouth right behind your upper front teeth, where it should remain for the entirety of the exercise. Then:

1. Exhale fully through your mouth and make an audible *whooshing* sound.
2. Close your mouth and inhale through your nose while counting to **four.**
3. Hold your breath and count to **seven**.
4. Exhale again through your mouth for **eight** counts.
5. Repeat this process three more times.

_____ **TRIED IT!**

MEDITATE

Problems that arise in our daily lives can seem huge and even insurmountable at times when really they just need to be approached from a new angle and mindset. Whenever you're hitting a wall of extreme frustration, try practicing the meditation below.

1. Take a few deep breaths and focus on the situation causing you stress.
2. In your head, tell yourself, "I will overcome this obstacle by viewing it differently, and I will be stronger because of it."
3. Take a few more deep breaths.
4. Shake your head and shoulders and visualize your stress flying out of your body.

_____ **TRIED IT!**

WRITE

Positive affirmations are powerful! Whenever you're feeling like you can't do something, like you're not worthy or otherwise down, grab a pen and paper and write notes to yourself like "I am always learning," or "I am capable, I am powerful, I am strong." You can also use the affirmation cards on the following pages. Tell yourself whatever you need to hear, and trust in yourself enough to believe it.

_____ **TRIED IT!**

LOUD AND PROUD

Cut out these affirmation cards, grab a family member or friend, stand in front of a mirror with them, and ask them to shout these phrases at the top of their lungs with you. Oh—is shouting not your thing? Then stick the cards on your mirror and say them softly to yourself as you get ready in the morning (alternate the one that you display). Works either way.

I TRUST MY
INSTINCTS.

I AM SMART,
BEAUTIFUL,
AND STRONG.

I WILL FIND
A WAY.

I SAY NO TO
DOUBTS AND YES
TO LIFE.

MY VOICE
MATTERS.

TBH, I'M A
ROCK STAR.

ZONE OUT

Set a timer for five minutes. Doodle. Enjoy.

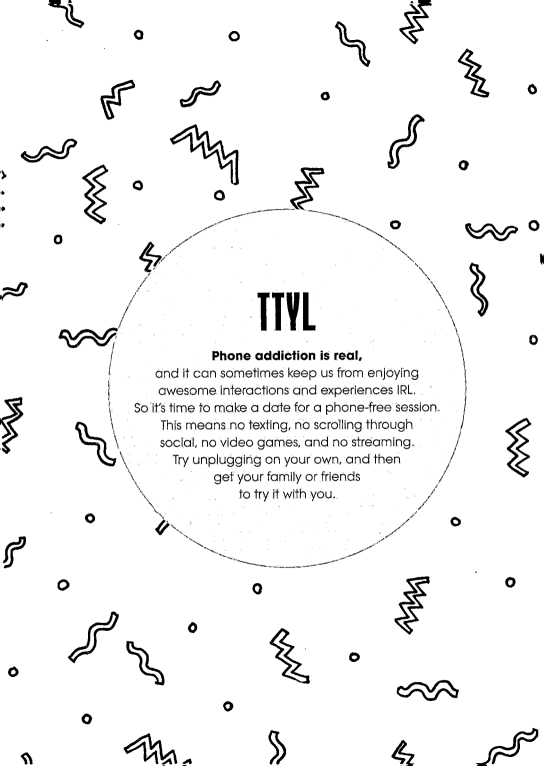

TTYL

Phone addiction is real,
and it can sometimes keep us from enjoying
awesome interactions and experiences IRL.
So it's time to make a date for a phone-free session.
This means no texting, no scrolling through
social, no video games, and no streaming.
Try unplugging on your own, and then
get your family or friends
to try it with you.

SOLO SESH

Spend an hour on your own without the phone (try doing chores, homework, a craft project, or just going for a walk). What did you do, and how did you feel afterward?

_____

_____

_____

_____

_____

GROUP DETOX

Arrange one night or afternoon with family or friends (board games, physical activities, cooking, and eating together encouraged). What did you do, and how did you feel afterward?

_____

_____

_____

_____

_____

BACK TO REALITY

Go to a public place (a café or a park), set your phone facedown onto this page, and trace its rectangular outline. Now watch other people and make note of any scents, noises, or things that get your attention. Jot them down or draw them outside of the rectangle. This is what you're missing out on when you're always looking down!

FLYING SOLO

Whether it's due to FOMO or an overloaded
plate, we can often neglect spending time
with the most important person in our lives:
ourself. Fill in the blanks with words or phrases
that complete the text based on your thoughts,
feelings, and personal experience. When
you're done, choose an afternoon to
spend with just yourself.

I know that I've spent too much time online when _____

_____ . At first, turning off my phone feels

_____ , but after a while I start to notice

_____ .

The thing that triggers FOMO the most for me is _____

_____ .

But I have to remind myself that saying no to _____

allows me to say yes to something that is more important to me: _____

_____ .

Being alone isn't being lonely. There's major _____

in solitude. I spend my downtime catching up on _____

_____ and indulging in _____ .

For me, the best recipe for self-care includes _____ ,

_____ , and plenty of _____ .

I have an ongoing resolution to _____ .

Ultimately, I'm my own greatest source of _____.

I am my own best company, and I don't require anyone's permission or

approval to enjoy myself.

THERE WILL BE TIMES YOU ARE SO SAD YOU CAN'T LIFT YOUR HEAD. AND THERE WILL BE TIMES YOU ARE SO HAPPY THAT THE SENSATION OF LIFE KNOCKS YOU DOWN. BUT MOST IMPORTANTLY, *THERE WILL BE YOU.*

SOLANGE KNOWLES

THE MAGIC THREE

Life wouldn't be the wonderful, dynamic, and fulfilling rollercoaster it is without highs that make your head spin and lows that teach you incomparable lessons. What's important is realizing that every day offers a chance to reframe what has happened previously.

What was the best moment of your day today (___/___/___)?

What was the most difficult moment of your day?

Come back a week later. What is your current perspective on those moments?

CHAPTER 06

RAISE YOUR VOICE

How will you be heard?

ASK YOURSELF: WHAT AM I WILLING TO FIGHT FOR?

KIMBERLY DREW

ACTIVISM IS AN EXERCISE IN STEPPING UP TO THE PLATE AND CURRENTLY, MILLIONS OF BRAVE TEENS ARE DOING SO. YOUNG PEOPLE AROUND THE WORLD ARE LEADING THE CHARGE BY STANDING UP FOR THEMSELVES, THEIR FRIENDS AND FAMILY, AND THOSE THEY DON'T KNOW BY DENOUNCING INJUSTICE AND DISCRIMINATION.

It's you and your peers **leading the walkouts**, planning the marches, **making the calls**, and **signing the petitions**. The causes you align with and injustices you want to rectify are up to you. Start by just picking one, and then figure out how you can get involved to the **best of your bandwidth** and ability. What contributions can you make within your own community?

Remember that **actions both small and large** count. Imagine what our world would look like if everyone did their little part to actively work toward a **brighter future**. Now more than ever, we have the ability to **influence one another**. Remember social change comes about when we decide—first individually and then collectively—**to think differently** about an issue. **Raise your voice** like only you can!

SIGN OF THE TIMES

Fill these signs with phrases or images relating to a cause you support or an issue you oppose. If a relevant rally is coming up in your area, make the sign IRL and march with it proudly above your head.

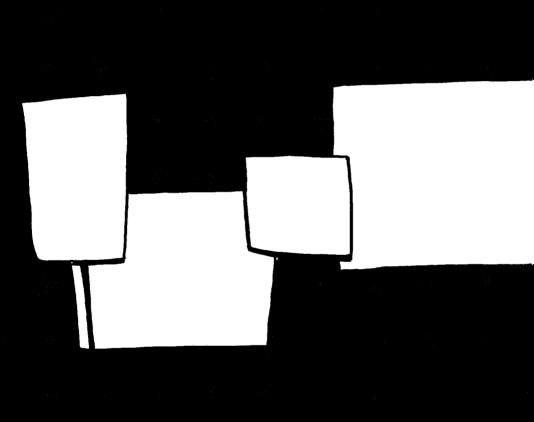

SAY IT LOUD

What would you say if you were given
the mic at a rally and were asked to speak
about a cause you care deeply about?
Imagine you had the ears of thousands of
people and fill in the blanks with the words
you'd want them all to hear.

Today, we all came out to this rally because we wanted our voices to _____. Freedom of speech is a _____ and it's important we _____ it.

I want to use that freedom to talk about _____. I personally care about it deeply because_____.

Supporting _____ is so important to our society and country because _____.

If we don't pay attention to it, repercussions could include _____ _____.

I think that people are afraid, apathetic, or hesitant to do anything about this issue because _____.

I deal with those feelings within myself by _____.

If I'm not able to do anything else, one small thing that I can do each day to further this cause is _____.

I believe that things can change if we are willing to approach each other with _____ and _____.

I can see a future where _____.

STEP UP

Think about a cause that you care deeply about, whether it's animal welfare, reproductive rights, or the environment. Search online for a relevant volunteer opportunity in your area. Reach out to your chosen organization, shelter, or campaign and arrange a day to volunteer with them. Check back in and write about your experience here.

POWER PLAYERS

National elections get the most attention, but citizens have the most direct voting power **at the local level,** where government policies have an immediate effect on the community. Local politics have **a trickle-up effect** on the national agenda. Even if you don't vote yet, you can start to see your role in the system by understanding which **elected officials require your vote.**

Search online for your voting district and write down the key people who represent you. If you live in the United States, you can start at **www.usa.gov/election-office** to find your local elections site.

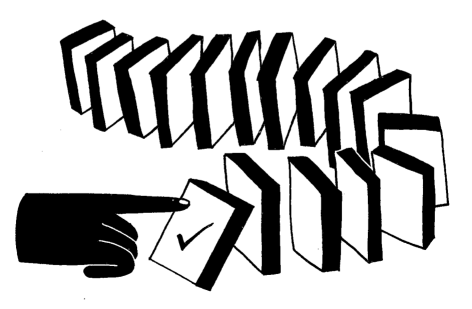

name:

position / party:

platform:

contact info:

name:

position / party:

platform:

contact info:

name:

position / party:

platform:

contact info:

name:

position / party:

platform:

contact info:

name:

position / party:

platform:

contact info:

name:

position / party:

platform:

contact info:

PERSONAL HERO

Write a letter to an important political
or social figure you admire (historical or current)
to tell them how and why their work inspires you.
If you ever feel discouraged or in need of some
motivation, flip to it, read it, and continue on
with a refreshed sense of determination.

DEAR _____ ,

_____

_____

_____

_____

_____

_____

_____

_____

_____

_____

_____

_____

_____

HIGHEST REGARDS, _____

DATE _____ **/** _____ **/** _____

YOUR VOICE IS POWERFUL. IF WE DON'T PROTECT THE MOST VULNERABLE AND MAKE IT CLEAR THAT IT'S UNACCEPTABLE TO STIGMATIZE PEOPLE, THEN WE'RE NOT LIVING UP TO THE BEST OF AMERICA.

LORETTA LYNCH

THE MAGIC THREE

How will you be the best citizen you can be? What efforts will you make to exercise your rights in support of marginalized people, causes you support, or issues you care about? Answer the questions below to remind yourself that we each play an ongoing role in shaping our society.

An example of one past injustice that truly shocks and enrages me:

1

One area where I feel our culture or government needs to change:

2

A sign of progress that excites me and gives me hope:

3

CHAPTER 07

FUTURE THINK-ING

What are your dreams and goals?

CLEO WADE

YOU HAVE THE ABILITY TO MAKE YOUR WILDEST DREAMS INTO REALITY. WHERE YOU'LL LIVE, WHAT YOUR CAREER WILL BE, WHO YOU'LL HANG OUT WITH, WHAT YOU'LL INVEST YOUR TIME IN, HOW MANY FRENCH BULLDOGS YOU'LL OWN, WHAT KIND OF PERSON YOU'LL BE—IT'S ALL ULTIMATELY IN YOUR HANDS.

Will the path toward achieving your goals be easy? Probably not. But what's a journey **without a little challenge**? When it comes to your life and what you want out of it, **be bold** and be imaginative. Dream huge, aspire for **peak happiness**, and never shortchange yourself with self-imposed limits.

This chapter is meant for **dreaming**. For taking all of your biggest hopes and goals and desires for your future and putting them into one place, no matter how **improbable or grandiose** they might seem. You'll be asked to think about what it is you want to achieve during your life and what you want it to look like **ten years from now**, while keeping your **role models** and what makes them so admirable in mind. When you work on the following exercises, approach them with the mentality that **anything is possible**. Because it is.

BUCKET LIST

What do you want to do before you die? Fill these pots and planters with your biggest goals.

YOUR PATH

Your true calling is out there, even if you don't
know what it is yet. That's totally OK. The things
you are good at and curious about now are
trail markers that you should follow until the day
you are doing work that suits and fulfills you.
Fill in the blanks to start sketching out
what this dream job could be.

People tell me that I'm good at _____ . They might

assume it comes to me naturally (and maybe it does), but I've also worked at

it by _____ .

At school, my favorite subjects are _____ .

Recently, I learned about _____ , and I found myself

wanting to know more. When I'm working on a school project, I get the most

satisfaction at the _____ stage.

In a group-project setting (in school or in an after-school activity), the role I

usually play is _____ , and I feel

_____ about it.

During my free time, the hours fly by when I'm _____ .

I love it because _____ .

A job that looks really cool to me is _____ .

If I knew (or someday meet) someone who does something similar, one thing

I'd want to ask about is _____ .

In my dreams, _____ would take me under their wing, but one

person who could mentor me right now is _____ .

I think I would enjoy helping people by _____ .

The world needs more _____ ,

and I'm confident I can bring that to the table.

COMIC RELIEF

Use the storyboard as a guide to create a one-page comic with you, ten years from now, as its central character. Think of this as your goal life and fill it with details indicating your dream home, job, friends, and hobbies*.

BOX 1: RISE & SHINE:
What does your ideal morning routine look like?

BOX 2: YOU BETTER WERK:
What do you fill your days doing, and how does it make you feel?

BOX 3: AFTER HOURS:
What do you fill your weekday evenings with?

BOX 4: WEEKENDS:
What do you do on Saturday and Sunday?

*If you don't want to draw elaborate scenes, you can draw stick figures with word bubbles, or just doodle objects and write captions.

A DAY IN THE LIFE OF

_____

NAME

_____

YEAR

SUPER YOU

Create your own superhero alter ego.

1. DESCRIBE YOUR POWERS.

You could choose one special trait of yours (could be anything, like being incredibly organized or a good listener) and then exaggerate it to superhuman levels:

_____

_____

_____

_____

_____

2. GENERATE A SUPERHERO NAME.

If you're stuck, try the following formula:
Honorific (Lady, Mistress, Princess, Doctor, Queen, Her Excellency, Boss, etc.)
Favorite Activity (Sleeping, Painting, Binge-watching, Selfie-taking, etc.)
Spirit Animal (Tigers, Sloths, Llamas, Chihuahuas, Narwhals, Unicorns, etc.)

_____ **of the** _____ _____
HONORIFIC   FAVORITE ACTIVITY   SPIRIT ANIMAL (PLURAL)

3. WHAT KIND OF COSTUME WOULD BEST SUIT YOUR SUPERHERO?

Design it on the figure opposite, using your favorite colors and symbols (cape and mask are not required—feel free to get creative).

Finish the piece by writing your superhero name and tagline on top.

I'M A HUMAN. I WILL MAKE MISTAKES. I WILL CHANGE MY MIND. I WILL FIGURE THINGS OUT AS I GO.

SASHA LANE

THE MAGIC THREE

Dreaming about your future is the easy part. Ensuring you get there in a way that's authentic to you and makes you feel happy, whole, and satisfied is more difficult. Remember that you will always be a work in progress, and that you'll probably need to renew the same goals and learn the same lessons multiple times.

I want to start:

1 _____

I want to stop:

2 _____

I want to continue:

3 _____

CONCLUSION

THIS IS NOT THE END

Where will you go from here?

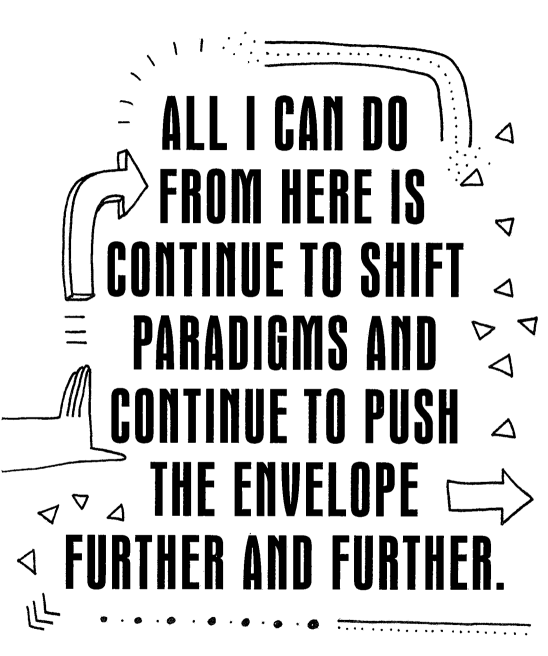

ALL I CAN DO FROM HERE IS CONTINUE TO SHIFT PARADIGMS AND CONTINUE TO PUSH THE ENVELOPE FURTHER AND FURTHER.

WILLOW SMITH

SO, YOU'VE DONE IT! YOU'VE REACHED THE END OF OUR GUIDE TO CONQUERING THE WORLD, MEANING YOU'RE PROBABLY MERE DAYS AWAY FROM TOTAL DOMINATION.

OK, maybe not quite. But hopefully you do feel more prepared to take on **whatever comes your way**. A few things to remember as you embark upon your journey of **living your dreams** and doing exactly **what YOU want to do**:

1. Pace yourself. Be deliberate and don't spread yourself too thin.

2. Have integrity. Stay focused on what is motivating you, and less on what everyone around you is saying or doing.

3. Failure is OK. It's inevitable. From failure, you learn, grow, and realize what needs to change as you move on.

4. Stay curious. There are always new things to learn and new ways to be. Staying open will bring you closer to achieving your dreams!

You are the future. Give yourself a huge pat on the back and go forth with **hope** and **determination** in mind.

SINCERELY, ME

Write a letter to your future self, ten years from now.
Tell this older version of yourself what you're doing right now, and what you're anxious about. Then ask your older self some questions—anything that you are most curious to know. End the letter with a word of advice for your older self, something essential that you don't want to forget. Someday, that piece of youthful advice might be exactly what your older self needs to hear!

DEAR _____,

_____

_____

_____

_____

_____

_____

_____

_____

_____

_____

_____

_____

_____

_____

_____

LOVE, _____

DATE _____ / _____ / _____

Design by Diane Shaw
Illustrations by Joni Majer
ISBN: 978-1-4197-3394-9

Printed and bound in China
10 9 8 7 6 5 4 3 2 1

ABRAMS The Art of Books
195 Broadway, New York, NY 10007
abramsbooks.com

MIX
Paper from
responsible sources
FSC
www.fsc.org   FSC™ C144853